VENUS WILLIAMS

A Real-Life Reader Biography

John Bankston

Mitchell Lane Publishers, Inc.

P.O. Box 619
Bear, Delaware 19701
http://www.mitchelllane.com

Mitchell Lane
PUBLISHERS

Printing   1   2   3   4   5   6   7   8   9

Real-Life Reader Biographies

Paula Abdul	Christina Aguilera	Marc Anthony	Lance Armstrong
Drew Barrymore	Tony Blair	Brandy	Garth Brooks
Kobe Bryant	Sandra Bullock	Mariah Carey	Aaron Carter
Cesar Chavez	Roberto Clemente	Christopher Paul Curtis	Roald Dahl
Oscar De La Hoya	Trent Dimas	Celine Dion	Sheila E.
Gloria Estefan	Mary Joe Fernandez	Michael J. Fox	Andres Galarraga
Sarah Michelle Gellar	Jeff Gordon	Virginia Hamilton	Mia Hamm
Melissa Joan Hart	Salma Hayek	Jennifer Love Hewitt	Faith Hill
Hollywood Hogan	Katie Holmes	Enrique Iglesias	Allen Iverson
Janet Jackson	Derek Jeter	Steve Jobs	Alicia Keys
Michelle Kwan	Bruce Lee	Jennifer Lopez	Cheech Marin
Ricky Martin	Mark McGwire	Alyssa Milano	Mandy Moore
Chuck Norris	Tommy Nuñez	Rosie O'Donnell	Mary-Kate and Ashley Olsen
Rafael Palmeiro	Gary Paulsen	Colin Powell	Freddie Prinze, Jr.
Condoleezza Rice	Julia Roberts	Robert Rodriguez	J.K. Rowling
Keri Russell	Winona Ryder	Cristina Saralegui	Charles Schulz
Arnold Schwarzenegger	Selena	Maurice Sendak	Dr. Seuss
Shakira	Alicia Silverstone	Jessica Simpson	Sinbad
Jimmy Smits	Sammy Sosa	Britney Spears	Julia Stiles
Ben Stiller	Sheryl Swoopes	Shania Twain	Liv Tyler
Robin Williams	Vanessa Williams	**Venus Williams**	Tiger Woods

Library of Congress Cataloging-in-Publication Data
Bankston, John, 1974-
     Venus Williams / John Bankston.
         p. cm. — (A real-life reader biography)
     Summary: A biography of the young tennis player who has been ranked among the top ten women players in the world.
     Includes index.
     ISBN 1-58415-129-3 (lib. bdg.)
     1. Williams, Venus, 1980—Juvenile literature. 2. Tennis players—United States—Biography—Juvenile literature. 3. African American women tennis players—Biography—Juvenile literature. [1. Williams, Venus, 1980- 2. Tennis players. 3. Women—Biography. 4. African Americans—Biography.] I. Title. II. Series.
GV994.W49 B36 2002

                          2002066069

ABOUT THE AUTHOR: Born in Boston, Massachussetts, **John Bankston** began publishing articles in newspapers and magazines while still a teenager. Since then, he has written over two hundred articles, and contributed chapters to books such as *Crimes of Passion,* and *Death Row 2000,* which have been sold in bookstores across the world. He has written numerous young adult biographies, including Mandy Moore and Alicia Keys (Mitchell Lane.) He currently lives in Portland, Oregon.

PHOTO CREDITS: Cover AP Photo/Alastair Grant; p. 4 Gary M. Prior/Allsport; p. 7 Ken Levine/Allsport; p. 10 Duomo/Corbis; p. 13 Ken Levine/Allsport; p. 17 Ken Levine/Allsport; p. 19 Reuters/Mark Baker; p. 22 Sean Garnsworthy/Getty Images; p. 23 AP Photo/Mark Lennihan; p. 25 Dylan Martinez/Reuters; p. 30 Alex Livesey/Allsport

ACKNOWLEDGMENTS: The following story has been thoroughly researched, and to the best of our knowledge, represents a true story. While every possible effort has been made to ensure accuracy, the publisher will not assume liability for damages caused by inaccuracies in the data, and makes no warranty on the accuracy of the information contained herein. This story has not been authorized nor endorsed by Venus Williams.

Table of Contents

Chapter 1
A Father's Dream

It was 1978, and Richard Williams was watching television. A tennis tournament was just concluding. Richard wasn't that interested in the player's athleticism or the game's outcome. What caught his attention was the oversized check presented to the winner. It was for over $30,000 - more money than Richard had earned all year. That was the day he decided his children should become tennis players.

Richard Williams was raised by a single mother with four other siblings. As far as Richard was concerned, the only mistake his mother ever made was marrying his father, a man who deserted his family. In spite of the obstacles she faced, Richard's mother

Richard Williams was raised by a single mother with four other siblings.

worked very hard to raise her children properly. One of his mother's lessons, more than any other, stayed with Richard his whole life.

One night, after a long day working in a blistering hot Louisiana field, Richard's mother asked him an important question. How would he feel if he had to work that hard all day, every day, for the rest of his life? Richard knew he wouldn't want to carry on that way. His mother's question helped him realize the importance of a good education.

He was pursuing that education in southern California when he met Oracene. She was a nurse from Mississippi who also came from a large family of eight children. After they married in 1972, the couple worked hard to develop several businesses in Long Beach, California, including a janitorial service and a security guard firm. They soon enjoyed a comfortable middle class life. Despite their financial success, the Williams chose to move their young family to one of the toughest neighborhoods in the United States.

Venus Ebone Starr Williams was born on June 17, 1980 in Lynwood, California. Before she was three years old the Williams family moved to Compton. Richard has told reporters he wanted his children to grow up tough. With that in mind, he picked the right place.

Compton is probably as well-known a part of Los Angeles as Beverly Hills or Malibu, but unlike those more desirable places, Compton's fame comes from its reputation for violence. This is due primarily to the large numbers of gangs in Compton, and the south central section of Los Angeles where it's located. While Compton is more dangerous than most neighborhoods, it is also a close-knit community. Quite a few successful business

Venus with her racquet at the age of ten

people, athletes, and hip-hop artists grew up there, but a star tennis player never hailed from Compton. Richard Williams hoped to change that.

Before Venus's birth, her father already had given her older sisters a try at tennis. Yetunde, Isha and Lyndrea eventually found success in other areas, but tennis was not for them. Venus was different. Both she and her younger sister Serena, who was born September 26, 1981, began tennis training as preschoolers.

"The first time I knew Venus was going to be a good tennis player was the first time I took her out on her very first day," Richard Williams told *Ebony Magazine*. "I was working with some other kids and had a shopping cart that would hold 550 balls. It took three kids who were teenagers a long time to hit those balls. They wanted to take breaks. Well, while they were taking a break, Venus wanted to hit every ball in that basket. She wouldn't stop. Every time you tried to stop her, she would start crying. She was only four years old."

While Venus showed promise in tennis from an early age, she faced several obstacles, besides coming from Compton. Spectators often view tennis as a sport

Both Venus and her younger sister Serena began tennis training as pre-schoolers.

primarily for affluent Anglo athletes. Even though African American athletes, such as Arthur Ashe and Althea Gibson, broke the so-called "color barrier" in tennis, African Americans players were still quite rare.

Even more uncommon were players from families without the extra money to help them succeed. Tennis can be an expensive sport. The costs for private lessons, coaches, club fees and dues add up quickly. While Richard Williams built a solid middle-class business, he couldn't afford these extra costs. What he lacked in money, he made up for with ambition. Richard poured his energy and every free minute into learning everything about the sport he could. He read about tennis in books. He watched matches on television. He reviewed video tapes of star players. By the time Venus was old enough to hold a racquet, her father knew a great deal about the sport.

Unfortunately, Venus didn't just lack a coach. She also lacked access to a professional tennis club. She began her tennis training on a public court in Compton. The court was poorly maintained with chips and ridges on the surface, and often littered with garbage and broken glass. Worse still, it was dangerous.

What Richard Williams lacked in money, he made up for with ambition.

Venus at the 2000 French Open

Fights between rival gang members near the tennis courts made them seem like a war zone. Richard often had to ask some of them to let his daughter use the court. Eventually he began tutoring a number of younger gang members, and later the gangs left Venus and Serena alone.

Venus developed quickly as a tennis player. In interviews she has admitted she was the type of young girl who wanted to be good and do what she was told. Pleasing her father made her happy. Still, that would never have made her succeed if she didn't have a combination of natural ability and drive that she showed even as a little kid. Despite her talent, when Venus Williams was five years old, her father told her she had to stop playing tennis.

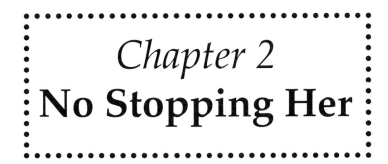

Chapter 2
No Stopping Her

Richard Williams dreamed of tennis stardom for his daughter Venus. Unfortunately she embraced the sport even more than he could have expected. While her enthusiasm was impressive, Richard worried she liked tennis too much. He wanted her to be well-rounded. He knew getting a good start on her education was important. If she got used to focusing on playing tennis all the time, her school work eventually would suffer.

Even though she was only five years old, Richard Williams took Venus' tennis racquet away. The decision was difficult, but it seemed like the right one. Venus began spending more time reading and playing

Richard wanted Venus to be well-rounded and worried she liked tennis too much.

with her friends, but her interest in tennis didn't fade easily. A year later, when Venus returned to the broken-down tennis court on the corner of East Compton and Atlantic Boulevard, she still longed to play. Her father relented, and allowed Venus and Serena to return to the sport they loved.

His decision wasn't easy. The courts were in a dangerous part of Los Angeles. One day while Venus and Serena were practicing, a gang member fired on the court. The girls were unharmed. Richard wanted his daughters to keep the incident a secret, but little Serena and Venus couldn't wait to tell their mom. They were too young to understand how much danger they'd been in. To the girls the shooting was just an exciting story.

Oracene was horrified. She forbid her husband to ever take the girls to the courts again. Only later did he manage to change her mind, convincing her that Compton was their neighborhood now. Making the place better was up to them. Richard did his part by setting up a business that offered low-cost health insurance to Compton residents. Sometimes improving Compton's image seemed to rest mainly on the slim shoulders of the Williams sisters.

Southern California has produced a legion of tennis champs from Billie Jean King to Pete Sampras. But to many the very idea of a tennis champ hailing from south central Los Angeles seemed ridiculous. Because of the media's poor perception of the area, Richard didn't just have to be a good coach, he also needed to be a good publicist. Celebrities often hire publicists to speak to the press and talk up their accomplishments. The Williams sisters weren't celebrities, but their father sure acted like they were. Before Venus was even 10 years old Richard talked regularly to reporters from local newspapers and

Venus and her sister Serena with their father in 1992

At 10 years old, Venus Williams was ranked number one, not only in her age group, but also among girls two years her senior.

television stations about her tennis prowess. Even then, he was controversial. Tennis professionals couldn't understand why he insisted on training the girls himself. After all, he'd never coached a professional tennis player before. Just wait, he thought, Venus will someday be the number one player in the world.

The idea seemed ridiculous. Number one? *Venus Williams?* But by 1990, the idea almost seemed possible. Over the course of a single year, Venus won 30 titles on the junior circuit. She won every tournament she entered. At 10 years old, Venus Williams was ranked number one, not only in her age group, but also among girls two years her senior. She was getting national attention.

The family needed to make a difficult decision. Even Richard was wondering if the time had come to hire a professional coach, maybe even enroll the girls in a tennis academy. Should they stay in Compton or move on? Had the time come to take the young tennis-playing sisters the press dubbed the "ghetto Cinderellas" out of the ghetto?

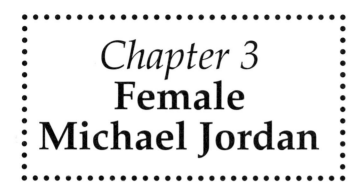

Chapter 3
Female Michael Jordan

Richard Williams didn't want tennis to be the most important thing in his daughters' lives. He wanted them to put school, family, and their church before playing tennis. The Williams are Jehovah's Witnesses, a faith that is very strict. Oracene and Richard met in church, and they wanted their faith to be important to their children as well.

Because her parents wanted her life to have balance, Venus only trained a few times a week, for a few hours at a time. At her age, many other girls who dreamed of becoming professional tennis players already trained six hours a day, six days a week. Besides the desire for a well-rounded life, part of the reason for Venus's schedule

Venus only trained a few times a week, for a few hours at a time.

had to do with Richard. He still needed to make a living. He only could coach his daughters during his free time.

In 1991, Richard realized he had taken Venus' tennis ability as far as he could, and he should turn her training over to more capable hands. Richard convinced Rick Macci, one of the best tennis coaches in the world, to fly from Haines City, Florida to Los Angeles. Richard tried to assuage Coach Macci's fears about visiting Compton by telling him, "You won't get shot."

When Macci arrived, Venus' tennis playing did not impress him. He had seen better. Venus was a lanky 10-year-old with more enthusiasm than technique. Ironically, Venus' athleticism caught Macci's attention during a break when she walked on her hands across the battered court, then did a flip and a few cartwheels. The display showed Macci how much raw talent the pre-teen Venus possessed. Macci later told friends he'd just seen the "female Michael Jordan." That day he offered both Venus and her sister Serena full scholarships to his tennis academy in Florida.

Still, Richard Williams wasn't satisfied. He used his security firm contacts to do a full background check on the coach, and for

In 1991, Richard realized he should turn Venus' training over to more capable hands.

several hours he asked the man more than five dozen questions. Richard didn't care that Macci was one of the best-known tennis coaches or that he was offering the Williams sisters an incredible opportunity. Venus and Serena were Richard's little girls; he wanted to make sure they'd be safe.

12 year old Venus practices on a court in Florida

Although Richard eventually realized he could trust Macci, he still wasn't willing to let Venus and Serena go to Florida on their own. Soon after the meeting with Macci, Richard sold his business, and the entire family relocated.

In Florida, Venus's life changed rapidly. Ocacene decided not to send her daughters to public school, but home schooled them instead. Venus' training also became much more intense. She soon followed the same regimen as many other aspiring professional tennis players, practicing six hours a day, six days a week. Richard Williams began worrying again. He feared the intense training and competing in tournaments would be too much for his daughters.

Richard had watched other young professional tennis players who trained six hour a day, six days a week along with tournament play from the time they were children. As teenagers, injuries often racked their bodies. Richard wanted his daughters to be healthy. This desire prompted him to keep them from entering junior tournaments.

Richard also wanted his daughters to avoid the stress of turning professional too early. His plan was for Venus and Serena to continue their education, train part time, and only become professional tennis players when they were ready.

From the time she was age 10 until she was 14 years old, Venus focused on her training. In many ways being out of the public eye only made her more intriguing.

Stories about Venus made the front page of newspapers, sports magazines, and network television sports. By 1994 Venus Williams was probably the most famous tennis player who wasn't professional.

Eventually, the Women's Tennis Association (WTA) altered Richard William's plans. The WTA announced a new rule in 1994 that limited the number of professional tournaments players less than 18 years old

Venus celebrates at the 2002 Australian Open

could play. The rule would not go into effect until 1995. Venus was 14 then and very talented. She did not want any limits. She would have to turn pro before 1995 to avoid restrictions, and she had to work on her father to convince him of her decision.

Venus' father wasn't sure. He knew the pressures a pro could face. But he also respected and trusted his daughter. In the end, he let the rest of the family make the decision. They voted to let Venus go pro. At the age of 14 Venus Williams became a professional tennis player. As a 10-year-old she'd been a very successful amateur. The question was, did she have what it took to be a successful professional?

Chapter 4
Tricks and Treats

On Halloween in 1994, 14-year-old Venus Williams stepped onto a tennis court as a professional for the first time. It seemed like the whole world was watching. Reporters from major sports magazines were present; kids her age and younger crowded around her for autograph. Everyone wondered if she was ready.

While most of her competitors spent the previous few days in rigorous practice, Venus and her family visited Busch Gardens in Tampa, Florida. The next day they flew out to Oakland, California. Instead of going to a tennis court, Venus went to a school, speaking to inner city kids. Although Venus didn't win the Bank of the West Classic, her

Everyone wondered if Venus was ready to play as a professional.

Venus' serve is now legendary

first professional tournament, her skills proved she deserved to participate.

From her stamina to her backhand and forehand, Venus demonstrated the techniques her father had been bragging about for years, but her serve gained the most attention. In tennis a powerful and accurate serve can make the difference between success and defeat. If an opponent can't return a serve, they can't win. Venus' serve eventually became legendary.

Just a few years after her professional debut, Venus became the fastest server in the history of women's tennis when a clock recorded her serve traveling more than 125 miles per hour!

Venus' combination of power and technique changed her family's life even before she became a highly ranked professional. Despite competing in only a third of the usual tournaments other teens her age played, Venus earned much more attention. Reebok, a top manufacturer of sneakers and athletic apparel, knew a winner when they saw one.

Venus was well-known for her beaded hair and streamlined clothing

Company representatives approached Venus and her family with an offer. Not only would she be a spokesperson for the product, appearing in ads and, of course, wearing the gear in competition, she also would help design her own line of tennis clothing. Venus had been experimenting with fashion design for a while. Even at age 15 she was almost as well-known for her beaded hair and tight streamlined clothing as she was for her serve.

The contract Reebok offered was worth 12 million dollars in 1995. By December 2000 the contract was renewed for an estimated 40 million dollars. The money changed the Williams' lives. They purchased a 10-acre estate in Palm Beach Garden, a middle class neighborhood near Palm Beach, Florida. Finally, their years of struggle and hard work had paid off.

In 1997, Venus earned her high school diploma with an A average. (She began attending private school in 1995.) Later, she took courses at a local college, the same year her tournament earnings topped $400,000. During 1997 she rose from the 211th best female tennis player in the world to the 26th best. She also became the first African American woman in nearly 40 years to reach the U.S. Open's finals (Althea Gibson competed in 1958.) By the late 1990s, members of the press finally were beginning to believe the prediction Richard Williams made when Venus was 10 years old. She wasn't number one yet, but each year she got closer.

Despite positive attention from the media, Richard Williams continued to be a controversial figure. After Serena turned professional, fans and media looked forward

Venus wasn't number one yet, but each year she got closer.

to an inevitable match between the two sisters. Yet every time the match appeared likely to happen, Richard would pull Serena out. Sometimes he said she was suffering from an injury, other times he blamed her grades. The press suspected he purposely was keeping his daughters from meeting on the tennis court.

In April of 1999, the match everyone had been waiting for happened. During the

Venus and her sister Serena at the women's doubles finals at Wimbleton in 2000

finals of the Lipton Championships in Key Biscayne, Florida the two sisters faced each other for the first time as professionals. The last time two sisters competed in a final tennis match was more than a century before —when Lillian Watson lost to her sister Maud in 1884.

The match between Venus and Serena was close, but Venus won: 6-1,4-6,6-4. When the match ended, Venus quietly walked to the net and gave Serena a hug. The two occasionally played against each other in tournaments over the next few years. Venus' extra years and extra inches continued to give her the advantage. (Venus is just over six feet tall and Serena is just under.)

After watching his two daughters play at the Lipton Championships Richard told the press, "I really thought I was going to cry. What was going through my mind was all the problems we've had in tennis, bringing the girls up, how difficult it was, the gang members, all the people out there. I was saying, 'Look where you are today.' It was so difficult for me to believe it."

Chapter 5
Big Mac Attack

England's Wimbledon Tennis Championship is the best-known tennis competition in the world. The courts attract the top tennis players in the world, while members of the British Royal Family and numerous celebrities watch from the stands. No matter how many tournaments a professional tennis player wins, no matter how many millions of dollars in endorsements they receive, tennis players aren't considered world-class champions until they win at Wimbledon.

The last African American to conquer the championship at Wimbledon was Althea Gibson, who won back-to-back championships in 1957 and 1958. Venus

Tennis players aren't considered world-class champions until they win at Wimbledon.

Williams was another trailblazer. Like Althea, Venus won back-to-back championships at Wimbledon in 2000 and 2001. (The trophy coincidentally is called the Venus Rosewater Dish.) Despite her two Wimbledon victories, and two back-to-back wins at the U.S. Open, Venus still wasn't the number one player in the world. In late 2001, that honor went to Martina Hingis, who hadn't won a major tournament in two years. "In my mind, I'm always the best," Williams said in 2001 after learning she was still number two.

Legally an adult, Venus appeared to step into her father's role of creating controversy. In interviews Venus Williams named a number of role models, including Gibson and John McEnroe, one of her favorite tennis players. McEnroe was a top player in the early 1980s famous for his antics on the court. He would yell at umpires and smash his racquet. While Venus generally was a disciplined player, in 1999 she appeared to learn about sportsmanship from the man once called "The Big Mac." During a match, some of her hair beads came loose, falling to the court. The second time it happened, the umpire penalized Venus a point for causing a disturbance.

"There's no disturbance! No one's being disturbed," she yelled at the umpire. When the referee refused to change his ruling, Williams became angrier, saying, "I don't think it's fair call." Later, fans booed her when she refused to shake hands with the umpire.

Although such outbursts are far more rare for Williams than they were for McEnroe, she earned the same type of negative press. One of her antics eventually caught the attention of "The Big Mac." The same year of the hair bead incident, Venus and her sister began saying they would be champions even if they played in the men's division.

In tennis, the question of whether or not women can compete against men has been asked repeatedly. In the 1970s, Billie Jean King, a top female player at the time, beat aging tennis pro Bobby Riggs. Certainly Venus, whose 167-pound frame is as muscular as any top male player, would be competitive against a man even with some top male players serving at 140 mph.

Billionaire real estate developer Donald Trump offered a million dollars to settle the question. The proposed match between Venus and McEnroe, however, never

Venus and her sister began saying they would be champions even if they played in the men's division.

Venus with her trophy from Wimbledon 2001

happened. McEnroe, despite being more than 20 years older than Venus, claimed to be up to the challenge. "Why in tennis do the women think they can beat the men?" McEnroe asked on a British radio station. "If they think that they should go and play in the men's tournaments, step up and play somebody."

The rivalry between McEnroe and Venus has continued over the last few years. In February of 2002, McEnroe repeated his challenge to Venus on the ABC television program *The View*. So far, Venus hasn't accepted. While the match could be interesting, it wouldn't be as exciting as one between a top male player her own age.

The question remains whether or not Venus, and the Williams family, have anything left to prove. In 2002, Venus Williams finally achieved the ranking Richard Williams promised when she was 10 years old. According to the February 24, 2002 WTA Tour rankings, Venus Williams was number one. But her number one standing was short-lived, when, in July 2002, her sister Serena kept her from winning her third straight Wimbleton and took over her spot as number one in the world. Serena won her second straight Grand Slam title. The all-Williams final was the first between siblings at Wimbledon since 1884, when Maud and Lillian Watson faced each other in hats and long dresses.

According to the February 24, 2002 rankings, Venus was number one. Serena took that title from her in July.

Chronology

1980   Venus Williams is born on June 17th in Lynwood, California
1983   the Williams family moves to Compton, California
1985   Richard Williams forces Venus to quit playing tennis for a year
1989   Richard Williams announces to the press that Venus would someday be the number one tennis player in the world
1989/1990 Venus is undefeated in the junior division. She wins 30 titles, and is ranked number one in both her age group and the 12-year-old group
1991   Venus and her sister Serena move to Florida and attend Rick Macci's Florida tennis academy.
1994   Venus becomes a professional tennis player
1995   Reebok offers a 12-million-dollar contract
1997   Venus graduates from high school
1999   Venus and Serena meet as professionals for the first time
2000   wins Olympic Gold Medal for both singles and doubles
2000/2001 Venus wins back-to-back Wimbledon Tennis Championships and U.S. Opens
2002   in February, the WTA ranks Venus Williams the number one female tennis player; in July, Serena ranks as number one after she won at Wimbledon

Index